C000147337

bray for insp

A Renaissance book

First published in 2006 by New Holland Publishers (NZ) Ltd
Auckland • Sydney • London • Cape Town

218 Lake Road, Northcote, Auckland, New Zealand
14 Aquatic Drive, Frenchs Forest, NSW 2086, Australia
86-88 Edgware Road, London, W2 2EA, United Kingdom
80 McKenzie Street, Cape Town 8001, South Africa

www.newhollandpublishers.co.nz

Copyright © 2006 in photography: Ian Baker
Copyright © 2006 New Holland Publishers (NZ) Ltd

ISBN–13: 978 1 86966 123 6
ISBN–10: 1 86966 123 0

Packaged for New Holland Publishers in 2006 by
Renaissance Publishing, Auckland
Design: Trevor Newman

A catalogue record for this book is available from
the National Library of New Zealand

10 9 8 7 6 5 4 3 2 1

Colour reproduction by
SC (Sang Choy) International Pte Ltd, Singapore
Printed in China through Phoenix Offset, Hong Kong

To the best of the packager's knowledge the inclusion of
quotations in this compilation falls under the fair use or
public domain guidelines of copyright law. If, however,
the packager has inadvertently made any error they would
be grateful for notification.

bray for inspiration

photography by IAN BAKER

NH
NEW
HOLLAND

You can't buy love, but you can pay heavily for it.

Henry Youngman

**Bees are not as busy as
we think they are.
They just can't buzz any slower.**

Kin Hubbard

Friendship is a mutual belief in the same fallacies, mountebanks, hobgoblins and imbecilities.

H.L. Mencken

Work is the refuge of those

who have nothing better to do. Oscar Wilde

To Americans English manners are far more frightening than none at all.

Randall Jarrell

You have to be born into country life to enjoy it – unless you're a cow.

Anon

A bore is a person who deprives you of solitude without providing you with company.

Gian Vincenzo Lavina

**There are three ways
to get something done:
do it yourself,
hire someone or
forbid your kids to do it.**

Monta Crane

**Depend on the rabbit's foot
if you will, but remember
it didn't work for the rabbit.**

R.E. Shay

Blame someone else and get on with your life.

Alan Woods

**Just remember,
once you're over the hill
you begin to pick up speed.**

Charles M. Schulz

**Sometimes I wonder
if men and women
really suit each other.
Perhaps they should live next door
and just visit now and then.**

Katharine Hepburn

**Principles are things with no
real force except when
one is well fed.**

Mark Twain

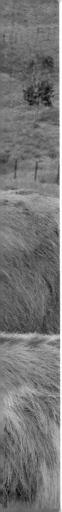

Committee: A cul-de-sac to which ideas are lured and then quietly strangled.

John A. Lincoln

You're not drunk if you can lie on the floor without holding on.

Dean Martin

Of all the 36 alternatives, running away is best.

Chinese proverb

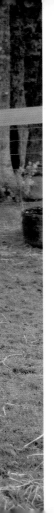

No animal should ever jump up on the dining-room furniture unless absolutely certain that he can hold his own in the conversation.

Fran Lebowitz

We come to love not by finding the perfect person, but by learning to see an imperfect person perfectly.

Sam Keen

The secret of success is sincerity. Once you can fake that, you've got it made.

Jean Giraudoux

Cough and the world coughs with you.

Fart and you stand alone. Trevor Griffiths

Collaboration is a word producers use. It means don't forget to kiss my ass from beginning to end.

Sam Shepard

I have not failed.
I've just found 10,000 ways
that won't work!

Thomas Edison

I refuse to think of them as chin hairs. I think of them as stray eyebrows.

Janette Barber

**Suburbia is where
the developer bulldozes
out the trees, then
names the streets after them.**

Bill Vaughan

Is marijuana addictive? Yes, in the sense that most of the really pleasant things in life are worth endlessly repeating.

Richard Neville

An honest politician is one who, when he is bought, will stay bought.

Simon Cameron

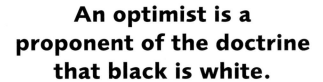

An optimist is a proponent of the doctrine that black is white.

Ambrose Bierce

All charming people have something to conceal, usually their total dependence on the appreciation of others.

Cyril Connolly

**A celebrity is one who is
known by many people
he is glad he doesn't know.**

H.L. Mencken

Were we closer to the ground as children or is the grass emptier now?

Alan Bennett

**Eternity's a terrible thought.
I mean, where's it all
going to end?**

Tom Stoppard

I backed the right horse and then the wrong horse went and won.

Henry Arthur Jones and Henry Herman

Statistics are figures that prove the best time to buy anything was last year.

Jack Benny

Admiration is our polite recognition of another's resemblance to ourselves.

Ambrose Bierce

A great many people think they are

thinking when they are merely rearranging their prejudices. William James

**Buy old masters.
They fetch a better price
than old mistresses.**

Max Aitken (Lord Beaverbrook)

Modesty is the gentle art of enhancing your charm by pretending not to be aware of it.

Oliver Hertford

I'm tired of all this nonsense about beauty being only skin-deep. That's deep enough. What do you want – an adorable pancreas?

Jean Kerr

If this raised a laugh, then try these
other Farmyard Wisdom titles:

Chewing the Cud
Fowl Play
Pig Tales
Wise Quacks
Woolly Wisdom